The Fifty Reasons Why It's Great to be a Man
© 2015 by Robert W. Brady, Jr.

ISBN: 978-0-9793679-2-2

This book is a work of fiction. Names, characters, places and incidents are products of the author's imagination or are used factiously. Any resemblance to actual events, locales or persons, living or dead, is entirely coincidental.

Cover art: Robert W. Brady, Jr.

Photography by JG Photos, Jason Good

First Printing

10   9   8   7   6   5   4   3   2   1

I can eat the same breakfast, lunch and/or dinner for six months in a row and not get tired of it

If I drop a comb in the toilet, I don't need a new comb.

I can go from asleep in bed with the pillow stuck to my head to suit, tie and shoes shined, walking out the door in 20 minutes.

If my best friend and I sit for 4 hours watching a football game and don't say a single word to each other the entire time, he is still my best friend.

If I go home with a girl I just met and do anything she wants, I will hear from her the next day.

When I buy a Harley this year, no one is going to assume I am gay.

I will never have to squeeze an object the size of a watermelon out of any orifice of my body

If I walk into a doctor's office and see stirrups, the only possible reason is that the doctor is a veterinarian

I am expected to belch without warning, scratch myself in public, drool and snore when asleep, and to gain weight as I age

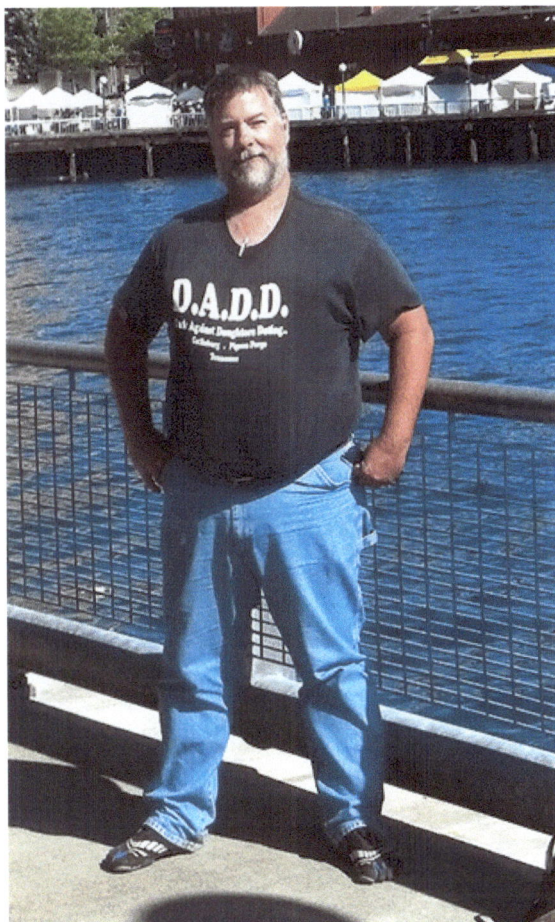

My best friend is a dog, and that is entirely ok

If I buy a pair of shoes, it is only because they are comfortable, and I just wore out a pair of shoes.

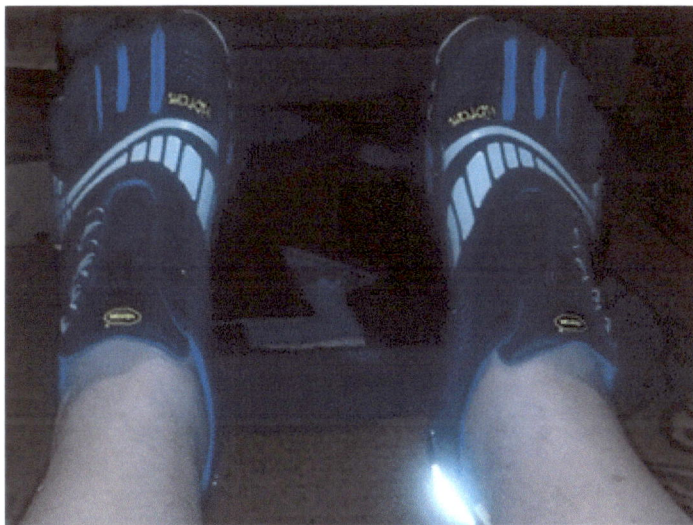

I can go to the beach in a bathing suit that makes me look fat and have a great time.

The more I sweat outdoors, working in
the sun, the sexier I become

If I fall in love with someone, I have the added benefit of knowing that, at least for a while, my kitchen will be clean

No one will ever ask me, "Can you put this in your purse?"

I can roll around in the lawn with the kids and the dogs, then go to a bank, supermarket or to dinner right after.

If I catch someone of the opposite sex checking out my butt, that is pretty darn cool.

If I get upset and get into a fight, I don't have to listen to some doofus making cat sounds.

I can act like a little kid sometimes without attracting perverts. In fact, my acting like a kid makes me more attractive to people of the opposite sex whom I would actually want to meet.

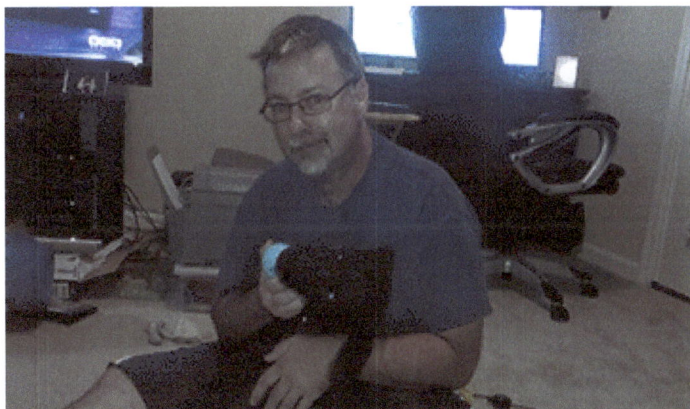

God granted me with the tone of voice
that terrifies young children

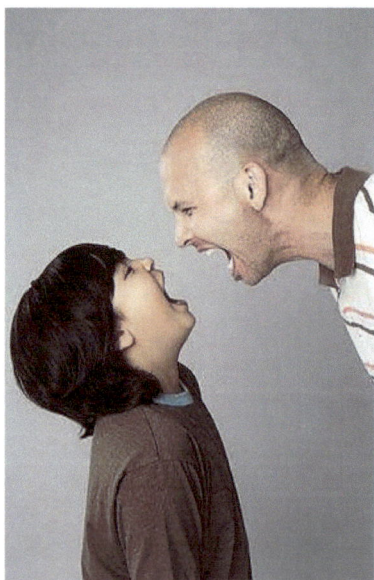

I buy shampoo on sale - in fact, the only reason I would even go into the hair care section of a supermarket is to walk by someone I wanted to check out.

A scar makes me look sexier

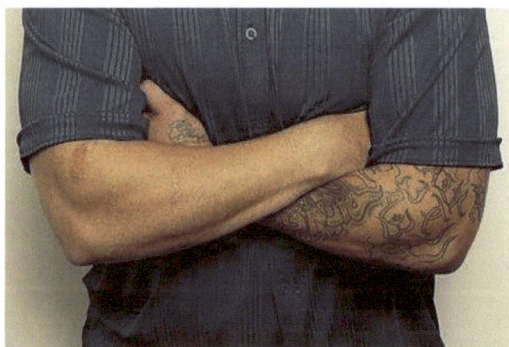

I realize I am bigger than a spider, a cockroach or a mouse, and therefore can defeat one in open combat.

No one is going to accuse me of
sleeping my way to the top

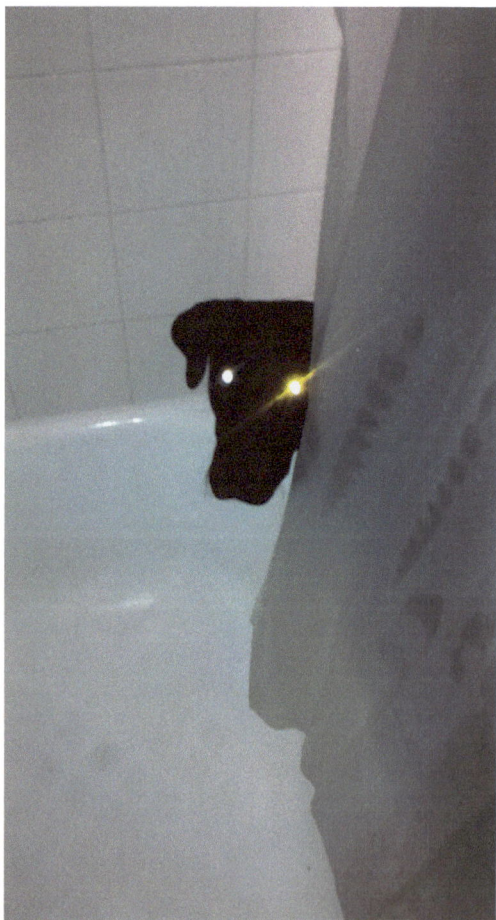

I know what tools do

I have no idea what a pain in the ass
pantyhose or makeup are

If I clean the house, it is a REALLY big deal

The only thing with wings I care about is an airplane

When I vote, I don't need to consider which candidate has better hair.

If I start dating a 19 year old, I am a hero

If someone says, "Did you hear what he/she said about him/her?" I get to honestly answer, "What do I care?"

No one is ever going to send me a cop-out gift of chocolate or flowers

My wallet goes with every single thing I own

Doing something that hurts actually
increases my self-esteem

Being able to cook is something about me that really impresses people

If I am hungry, I can eat practically anything, regardless of age, color or how hard it was to pry off of the surface it was sitting on

I get to pick my nose at stoplights

I buy underwear that's comfortable and I wear it until it actually dissolves, all for $9.95 a three-pack.

I can decide on food items, vehicles to buy, major surgery and/or where I want to go on vacation in under 60 seconds.

Having to kiss someone who forgot to shave doesn't hurt

Tuxedo: $65/night, I look great and I
don't care if someone else is wearing
the exact same one.

No one asks me if it is ok to make any decision

Being sexually harassed shows that I 'Still got it'

No matter how pissed off someone
makes me, I will likely not remember
why the next day or, if I do, I can resolve
the issue entirely with a beer.

All I have to do on Thanksgiving is eat and watch football

Every single card by Hallmark sounds exactly the same to me, so picking one takes about 15 seconds, and yet I get full credit for whatever it says.

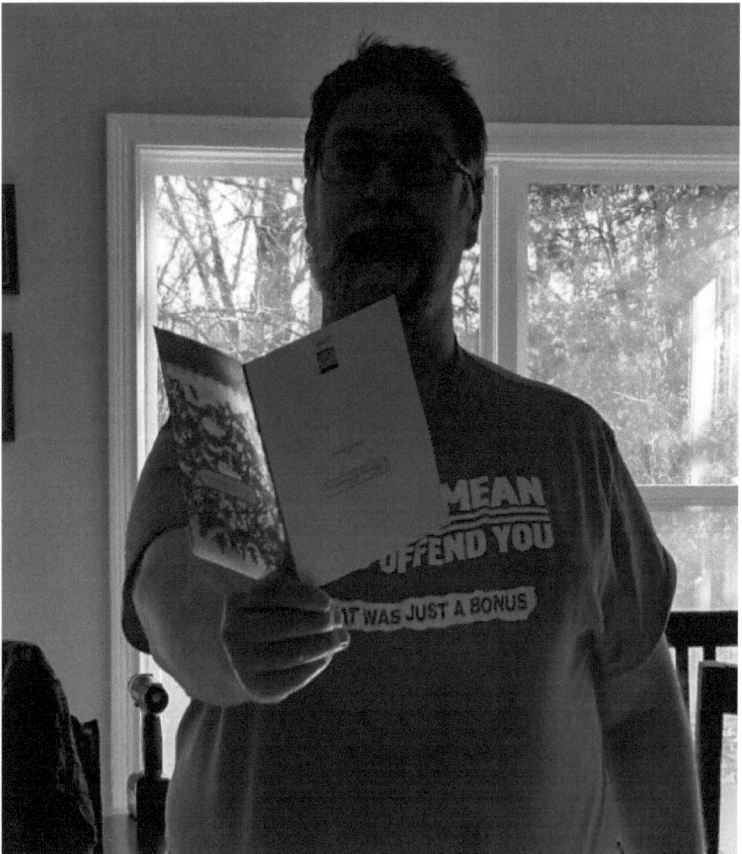

Break a nail? What's that?

I just don't care how long my eyelashes are

I get to wear old, worn, tattered shirts that make me feel like I am back in high school

And best of all:

I can write a book like this, that will be seen by thousands of people, and not one of them will think I am a bitch.

And now:

The Ten Secrets that No Woman Must Ever Know.

So, after you read this, for the love of God don't tell anyone!

After God created man, and named him Adam, and set him down to live the perfect life in the Garden of Eden, He came to Adam and told him, "Remove one of your own ribs, and I will make for thee the perfect companion, Eve."

"You want me to do *what* now?"

"Pull out your rib, Adam, that I might -"

"No, I heard you. Why the hell would I want a companion?"

"For that thou shalt multiply, and bring forth-"

"Yeah, that's what I thought. Pass."

And God's wroth was great, and He said, "Look, Adam, this is going to happen. Don't make me do to you what I did to the snake."

"Yeah, well, the snake says that that fight's not over. Look - this place is great, I am fine, and the bathroom seats one. We had the 'If something works, don't fix it' talk when you tried to turn the horse into a unicorn."

Predictably, God won, and Adam brought forth Eve from his own rib, and she immediately set forth to rearranging the furniture in Eden, and most unfortunately changed Adam's diet, because she felt it wasn't healthy for him.

"She served you WHAT?"

"I told you," Adam said, still chewing. "I was happy with

the river of malt beer and the popcorn bush."

"Oh, you two are *so* out of here!"

And Adam dropped his apple, and said, "What? What did I do?"

"Look Adam, this is going to be one of my truisms that you better get used to: no matter what she does, no matter how much you opposed it, when she screws up, YOU are going to be blamed for it, and pay a heavy price."

And Adam and Eve were exiled from Eden, and moved to the land of Nod, where the rivers were filled with water.

In time, Adam and Eve had two sons, Cane and Able and, when they were old enough, Adam took them aside.

"Look, guys - I am going to enlighten you to a few things, just don't tell your mother."

"Ever?" Cane asked.

"Never. In fact, don't tell any woman. One day in the distant future there will come one who will have the temerity and the wisdom to enlighten them, but until then, pass this on to your sons, and keep it our little secret."

For thousands of years, these ten things have been kept hidden from womankind, waiting for the time when the wisest of men deemed it fit to share them.

This is that time, I am that man:

The 10 Secrets that No Women Must Ever Know:

1. You know that thing you do, that you think you do better that any other girl? Well, every girl thinks that, and you're all wrong.

2. We don't actually like small, petite feet - we like the fact that we can get you to walk around all day in shoes that are too small.

3. We engineered the women's rights movement in order to trick you into thinking that you needed to work.

4. There is no article of clothing on the planet that even slightly affects the appearance of the size of your butt.

5. The only reason that we like sports so much is that you don't get it. The only reason that you don't get it is that, when we explain it to you, we slightly change the rules every single time.

6. The only reason that we check out other women is to piss you off

7. When we hold and comfort you on those days that you can't help but cry, we used to display the whole scene secretly in cave drawings, which is the original reason men did them. This evolved eventually to painting, television, moves and, finally, the Internet. Later we gather around these images and laugh about them.

8. Men who are willing to go out for tampons in the middle of the night are actually either seeing hookers or gambling.

9. We don't care if you put on weight once we marry you - we just like the idea that you have to watch us have three desserts and a six-pack while you slowly chew a carrot.

10. We don't really die younger than you do - we fake it and go to a secret island in the middle of the Pacific known as Beer and TV Land, where we live for another ten to fifteen years. No one has ever spoken a word on that island except during a commercial, and no one every will.

Now that you know - shhhhhhhhhhhhhhhh!

www.ingramcontent.com/pod-product-compliance
Lightning Source LLC
LaVergne TN
LVHW010022070426
835508LV00001B/10